Animals in the Forest

ANIMALS

in the
FOREST

RAINTREE PUBLISHERS
Milwaukee

This book has been reviewed
for accuracy by
Dr. Charles P. Milne, Jr.
Visiting Assistant Professor
Department of Biology
Marquette University, Milwaukee, Wisconsin

Copyright © 1988, Raintree Publishers Inc.

© 1986 Hachette, translated by Mark Inglin.

Library of Congress Number: 87-20689

   2 3 4 5 6 7 8 9 0   93 92 91 90 89

Printed and bound in the United States of America.

Library of Congress Cataloging in Publication Data

Animaux des bois et des forets. English.
   Animals in the forest.

   Translation of: Animaux des bois et des forets.
   Includes index.
   Summary: Describes birds, insects, snakes, deer, and
other fascinating creatures that make their homes in
the woodlands.
   1. Forest fauna—Juvenile literature. [1. Forest
animals]   I. Raintree Publishers   II. Title.
QL112.A5513   1987   591.909′52   87-20689
ISBN 0-8172-3110-0 (lib. bdg.)

CONTENTS

THE MARTEN

A DISCREET PRESENCE

The marten is a difficult animal to observe. It never comes close to where people live. It hunts at night, looking for food over a large territory. During the day it rests in holes in trees and in abandoned nests. Even so, it is found in all the great forest regions of Europe, Asia, and northern North America. It looks for a dark forest with huge trees in which to live.

The marten looks something like a weasel. It has a supple body and a sharp eye. The same size as a cat, the marten has a long and tufted tail and brown fur. A bright spot underneath the throat, called the bib, is yellow-orange. Its short legs end in big claws which help it climb. Adapted, above all, to living in the trees, the marten climbs better than a cat. It jumps from tree to tree, with leaps of more than two feet, and can climb down the trunk of a tree head-first. It is the only mammal able to chase down a squirrel in the branches of a tree. In many regions, the squirrel is its main food source, or prey. But the marten also eats other forest rodents, birds, eggs, and, less frequently, insects and berries.

In April, the female usually gives birth to two or three young that she suckles for six to eight weeks. At about three months, the young martens start to follow their mother in her hunting. They will stay with her until the fall.

It is rare to be able to observe the light tracks of the marten.

DIFFICULT TO FIND

The marten is one of the animals whose habits we know the least about. It is very wild. Its eyes, its ears, and its keen sense of smell allow it to detect other animals from very far away. Its tracks are not easy to follow. Since it is lightweight this animal does not make deep tracks. And because much of its life takes place in the trees, it leaves few traces of its tracks on the ground.

The marten's sense of hearing is so acute that it can even detect the noise made by mice. Its sense of smell is very sharp, and it sees in the darkest night. It is most successful when it hunts at dusk and during the night.

If the wind carries the scent of a squirrel sleeping in its nest to the nostrils of the marten waiting for game, the marten may climb to the top of the tree, make a hole in the squirrel's nest and devour the rodent quickly.

If the night is too dark, the squirrel will have no chance to escape. If it's a clear night, a frantic race will begin. The marten climbs and leaps from one branch to another along with the squirrel. It knows how to use its tail as a pendulum and a rudder. But the squirrel has its own tactics: it always climbs higher and higher, where the branches can no longer support the weight of the heavier marten.

A FRAGILE BALANCE

Squirrels are often the victims of the marten's appetite. Curiously though, it is when there are no longer any martens that the squirrels' population decreases.

The marten first attacks sick or weak squirrels. By killing these animals, the marten helps control sickness and disease in the squirrel population. Hunters blame martens for eating large numbers of game birds. But it should be remembered that in some countries, pheasants and partridges are raised like chickens and then released in the wild the day before a hunting party takes place. This ensures that guests will bring game back from the hunt. Since these animals do not know how to protect themselves in their new environment, martens and other meat-eating animals, or carnivores, have feasts on such days.

In the fall, the marten eats berries and fruit. In winter, it again becomes a carnivore and attacks birds and rodents which do not hibernate.

A VICTIM OF ITS BEAUTY

In the past, women of fashion wore fur scarves. Marten fur, which is especially beautiful and thick, was much sought-after. The marten was hunted or trapped during the winter, so much so that it disappeared from many forests.

Fascinated by an object left in its view, the marten is then easily observed . . . if we are not too close.

Today, in some parts of the world, it has become necessary to protect this animal, as well as the rest of the mustelidae family of mammals (otters, ermine, badgers, and polecats). These small mammals, in danger of extinction, contribute to the natural balance of nature in the forest.

THE HAWK

A FAMILIAR BIRD OF PREY

The hawk is a bird of prey. It captures live animals and kills them for food. Sometimes the hawk perches near the ground as it waits for some rodent to come near. At other times, it soars slowly, circling very high in the sky. Hawks have very good eyesight and can spot potential prey from a great distance. They are good fliers and can pounce with lightning speed on an unsuspecting animal.

The size and color of the hawk varies, depending on the kind, or species. There are about 260 kinds of hawks throughout the world. Usually, but not always, a male and female of the same species are similar in color. Often, the female is larger and more aggressive than the male. The hawk in the picture is a kind commonly found in Europe.

A CRUDELY-BUILT NEST

Hawks and other birds of prey raise their young in crudely-made nests called aeries. These loosely woven nests are made from twigs and grasses and lined with moss and leaves. They are built at the tops of very tall trees, or on cliffs and mountaintops. Usually the male and female build the nest together. They may return to the same nest year after year.

In spring, the female hawk lays from two to six eggs, depending on the species. She broods them, or sits on them to keep them warm, for about three to four weeks. When the young hawks hatch from the eggs they are quite helpless at first. The parent birds bring food to the nest. Using their strong beaks, they tear it apart and feed it to the young hawks.

11

A FIERCE HUNTER

It is possible to watch a hawk in its quest for food. If you spot a hawk perched on a fencepost or on a small shrub, stay still and watch it carefully. With its head buried in its shoulders and its feathers puffed out, it may seem to be sleeping. But its sharp, piercing eyes are constantly searching the ground for signs of prey. And suddenly, with one flap of its wings and with lightning speed, it will attack its victim — something it has spotted moving in the grass below.

Hawks have sharp, curved claws, or talons, for seizing their prey and carrying it away. With their strong, hooked beaks, they can easily tear apart the animals they capture.

Different kinds of hawks eat different types of animals. They may eat voles, moles, snakes, field mice, lizards, frogs, insects, and shellfish.

The hawk feeds basically on field and meadow rodents.

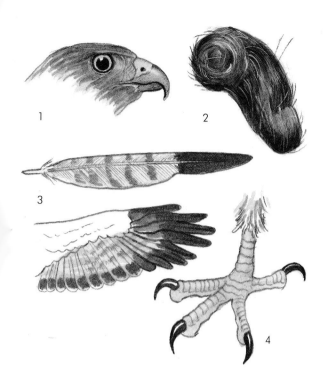

Hooked beak (1), undigested matter (2), long feathers (3), and sharp claws (4) characterize the birds of prey.

A MISUNDERSTOOD BIRD

Hawks are sometimes thought to be enemies of the farmer. That is because hawks sometimes raid chicken yards. In fact, in rural areas, hawks are commonly called "chicken hawks" for this very reason. Hawks also kill small birds and animals that are considered game animals by sportsmen. So it is not surprising that, in the past, farmers and hunters have intentionally killed hawks by either shooting them or trapping them.

THE BALANCE OF NATURE

But, like other animals, hawks play an important role in helping to maintain the balance of nature. By preying on mice and other small rodents, hawks help to keep the population of such animals in check. When this delicate balance of nature is disturbed in some way, the results can be very damaging.

An example of this occurred in Jura, France, just a few years ago. Hunters and farmers had killed so many hawks that there were none left in the area. Soon, farmers' fields were overrun by voles and field mice. When you consider that one vole will stockpile two pounds of wheat in its hole at harvesttime, you can imagine how great the crop loss was. The farmers tried several ways to control the rodent population. But none was successful. Finally, a pair of hawks was brought to the area. And the law forbidding the hunting of hawks was strictly enforced. Soon, the population of voles and field mice in the region began to decrease, as a pair of hawks can destroy about 6,000 voles per year. The farmers were happy because their crops were saved. And the balance of nature had been restored.

PROTECTED SPECIES

Many countries now have laws to protect hawks and other large birds of prey. In the United States, both the federal government and many state governments have issued such laws.

The Europeans also try to protect hawks in another way. On the freeways in heavily forested areas, there are road signs warning motorists that hawks and other birds of prey live nearby.

THE BOAR

A POWERFUL ANIMAL

The wild boar is the ancestor of the domestic pig. It lives in Asia, North Africa, and in some of the forests of Europe. The boar has a large, stocky body. Its big head has a long, movable snout and ears covered with rough hair. The wild boar has an excellent sense of smell and hearing. It has bright eyes, but its eyesight is poor. The boar has a mane on its strong neck that bristles when it is surprised or irritated. Its tail is movable and ends in a small tuft of hair.

The boar's color changes according to the seasons, from dark brown to light gray. In the fall it gets a thick fuzz, covered with long dark bristles. In the spring, the fuzz falls out and the bristles grow again, shorter and lighter.

Before winter, the boar accumulates a layer of fat underneath the skin. This serves as a supply of stored energy and also helps to protect it from the cold. The adult male has a very thick skin around the shoulders; this protects it from the biting attacks of its enemies.

A CARING MOTHER

At the end of the winter, the female, or wild sow, gives birth to two to six young boars in a nest made with grass, dead leaves and branches. The young are born with their eyes open and have a pattern of bright, dark stripes on their backs. They are able to follow their mother from an early age. She nurses them until they are two or three months old. The sow does not hesitate to attack other animals when she senses that her young are in danger.

KNOWING THE BOAR BETTER

The boar is a nocturnal animal, that is, it moves about mostly at night. During the day it cannot be easily seen because it stays hidden in thick brush. Usually it rests near a wallowing place, a shallow area hollowed out by its large body in a muddy pond. When taken by surprise, the boar flees. It is an excellent runner. With its short legs and solid hooves it can reach a speed of twenty-four miles an hour and can cover very long distances.

People are the main enemy of the wild boar in Europe. Boars may move from one living area to another if they sense that too many people are near.

Hunting wild boars has always been a favorite pastime in Europe. It is regarded as a noble sport, one that has been practiced by kings since the Middle Ages. Even today, wild boars are kept in the forests of some of the great estates in Europe and are hunted by sportsmen.

THE BOAR'S HEAD

The boar's head is very powerful, and its two sharp tusks make it a dangerous weapon. The snout and tusks are also useful in finding things to eat. Boars have a varied diet. They root around in the ground searching for plant roots and bulbs. The boar's keen sense of smell helps it to find acorns and earthworms beneath the ground. Next to ponds and marshes it buries its

An old male with its winter coat.

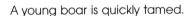

A young boar is quickly tamed.

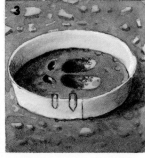

How to make a mold of an animal's tracks.
1) Remove stones and leaves from animal tracks,
2) Brush area with vegetable oil in order to
help in removing the mold later, 3) Make a frame
around the tracks with a circle of cardboard
buried in the ground, 4) Pour the plaster of
paris, 5) Let it dry for one hour, then remove from
the ground.

snout under the ground and uncovers reed roots, which it crushes with its powerful jaws. Boars also eat fruits, leaves, small animals, and birds' eggs.

The boar is a large animal; it may weigh more than 400 pounds, so it has a huge appetite. Sometimes wild boars are attracted to growing fields of grain, and they may do a lot of damage to farmers' fields. So, in some parts of Europe, the wild boar is considered a pest.

CUNNING AND INTELLIGENCE

Some sportsmen have brought boars to the United States to be hunted. But the boar is a highly intelligent animal and knows how to defend itself very well. If it does become trapped, it will turn and fight. This makes boar hunting a very dangerous sport.

TELLTALE SIGNS

It is possible to tell a lot about an animal by the kinds of signs it leaves behind it in the forest. Ground that has been rooted up is a good sign that wild boars have been there. So are trees which the wild boar has rubbed against to rid itself of parasites. The experienced woodsman can tell a lot about an animal by looking at its tracks — whether it is male or female, its weight, its age, its speed.

BARK BEETLES

STRANGE PATTERNS

In the thicket, a tree is dead. When the bark falls away, a strange pattern can be seen on the trunk of the tree. Both the elm tree and the ash tree have this pattern.

In the forest, an oak, a fir, a pine or birch tree are marked in a similar way. Little piles of sawdust in the cracks of the bark or at the foot of the tree mean that hungry insects are present. If you look more closely, you will notice that the designs created by these tiny wood carvers are different from one another. Each is the particular mark of a specific kind of insect. If you were to find a round hole in a tree trunk with tunnels leading out from it like the spokes of a wheel, you would know some insect had laid many eggs in the large round hole. When wormlike larvae hatched from the eggs, they ate their way out of their "nest." This is the work of bark beetles.

A VERY SMALL INSECT

There are many kinds of bark beetles, beetles which live in the wood or under the bark of trees. The kind, or species, of beetle pictured here is commonly found in Europe. The tiny adult insect is usually less than one-fourth of an inch long. It is brown or black and is shaped like a capsule. The female lays her eggs in the trunk of the tree; from each egg, a white, wormlike larva emerges. The larva eats heartily and grows quickly. Then it enters a pupal, or resting, stage. Finally, as an adult insect, it will pierce the bark and escape to the outside world.

SIGNS OF DANGER

In the forest, the bark of a fallen pine tree comes off in big strips. Patterns appear here and there on the inward surface of the bark; they are also on the surface of the wood. If you look closely, you will notice that the two halves fit together. Each groove is filled with sawdust where the wood has been eaten away.

If you place such a piece of bark in front of the sun, you can see that a ray of sunlight passes through a little hole. It is the opening to the central tunnel. From this tunnel other tunnels begin: the entrance to each tunnel is narrower than the outer end of the tunnel. If the tree fell not too long ago, you may discover a white maggot at the end of a tunnel. It is a larva. It came out of an egg laid at the tunnel's narrow entrance by a female bark beetle. She bored through the bark, dug the central tunnel, and laid as many eggs on both sides as there are side tunnels. The tunnel is larger at the outer end because as the larva grew, it needed more room. It made a bigger space for itself by eating away the wood.

To find out how many insects have laid eggs along a tree trunk, just count the designs. But remember that the presence of such patterns means that the forest is in trouble. Bark beetles only attack trees that are already weakened by lack of water, a serious injury, or pollution of one kind or another. Their attack is a death sentence for the tree because they eat its living wood.

The hole where the light is coming through marks the opening to the central tunnel.

Tracing the pattern of the bark beetles' tunnel.

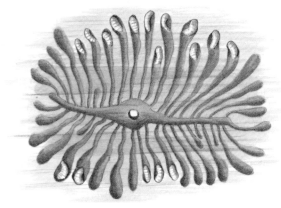

A CARRIER OF DISEASE

There are two kinds of bark beetles which have caused extensive damage to elm trees throughout Europe and in the United States. They are called elm bark beetles. One is native to Europe, the other to North America.

As the beetles bore into the tree, the fungi attack the tree's tiny pipelike vessels that carry water from its roots to its leaves. In order to defend itself, the tree produces special kinds of cells called tyloses. These block the vessels in an attempt to keep the infection from spreading. In a diseased tree, the blocked vessels prevent water taken in by the tree's roots from reaching its leaves. The leaves of the tree turn yellow and begin to fall off. Within a few weeks to several years, depending on the species, the tree will die.

AN INSECT INSIDE AN INSECT

Some insects use the bodies of other insects as nests in which to lay their eggs. Such insects are called parasites. Ichneumon wasps are parasites. They lay their eggs in the bodies of bark beetle larvae.

This is one way nature has of controlling the bark beetle population. Woodpeckers, nuthatches, and tree creepers also feed on bark beetles in their larval and adult stages.

Air pollution weakens the forest, the bark beetles settle in, the trees begin to die.

THE COMMON JAY

A RELATIVE OF THE CROW

The jay is a member of the crow family. But jays are smaller and more colorful than crows. The jay in the picture is commonly found in Europe. It has a brownish rose plumage. When it is flying, other colors can also be seen. Its wide rounded wings are marked with white and are partially covered by small blue feathers striped with black. The best known jay in the United States is the blue jay. It has striking blue and white feathers and a crested head.

The jay you see in the picture makes its home in oak forests. Its slightly hooked beak is strong enough to break twigs from the branches of trees. It arranges these in an untidy nest in the fork of a tree trunk or at the top of a small tree. The jay lines its nest with roots and dry grasses. It is a crudely made nest, but one which is well hidden.

In May, the female jay lays four to six eggs which are brownish green with brown spots. The eggs hatch in about fifteen days. The young birds are fed by their parents. They leave the nest about three weeks later, but stay with the family of jays until autumn.

While the jay is feeding its young, it catches an amazing number of wasps, crickets, spiders, caterpillars, and large beetles. In fact, during their stay in the nest, each of the young jays probably eats several thousand insects! Adult jays mostly eat various kinds of nuts and seeds.

In the fall, the jay picks or gathers acorns and carries them in a large storage space in its throat called the crop. It eats some of the acorns and buries the rest under moss or leaves. It sometimes visits these hiding places in winter when food is scarce, but often the jay seems to have forgotten where it has stored its acorns. And so, without knowing it, the jay helps in the planting of oak trees.

At this time of year, the jay also eats beechnuts, hazelnuts, fruits and wild berries.

The jay scatters acorns in the forest.

A SENTRY

Jays seldom leave the cover of the woods. Although they may be well hidden in the trees, you will know they are there because they make so much noise. Indeed, when they are gathered together in small flocks, jays seem to be trying to outdo one another with their noisy chatter!

Jays have loud, harsh voices. They often serve as a sort of sentry in the forest. Perched on a branch, with its neck craned forward and its crest raised, the jay will call out a loud warning if it sees or senses danger. Hunters are not fond of the jay because it alerts other animals in the forest to their presence.

A MIMIC

Jays are wonderful mimics. They can imitate the calls of many different birds.

At the first sign of danger, the jay gives the alert.

In the past, young jays fallen from the nest were often taken home and raised by farmers.

To build its nest, the jay looks for twigs, dry grasses, and small roots.

In the past, in the country, young jays that had fallen from the nest were often taken home by farmers and raised. Young jays raised in captivity make most amusing pets. Jays are curious by nature and soon become familiar with their new surroundings and "adopted" family. They seem to have a sense of humor and often learn to perform funny antics. Because they are such good mimics, jays may learn to imitate a cat's meowing if there is a cat around the house. And some jays raised in captivity have even learned to imitate certain words spoken by members of the household, much as parrots learn to talk.

AN OLD FOLK TALE

Sometimes it is possible to find a lovely blue jay's feather in the forest. The jay may have lost it in a fight with another animal or during the time it was shedding its feathers, or molting. If you find a feather in the woods, take it home and look at it closely. Its color is a very striking blue.

Why are the jay's feathers such a pure and lovely blue? According to an old European folk tale, all the snakes in the world would gather on a spring night, once a year, to make a fabulous blue diamond with their poison, or venom. One day the blue jay learned about this. It stole the snakes' diamond and took it home to its nest. Since then, according to the legend, the jay uses the beautiful blue from the stolen diamond to color its wings!

THE ASP

DISTINCT MARKINGS

The asp viper, commonly called the asp, is a poisonous snake that is found in most of western Europe, except in Spain. It lives in open meadows, on the plains, along hillsides, and in low-lying mountain regions. The asp prefers dry ground and open areas where it can sun itself.

Its colors and markings make the asp easy to recognize. It is yellowish brown to reddish brown, and the length of its body is marked with darker geometrical shapes. It measures 1½ to 2½ feet from head to tail. The asp's head is a definite triangular shape, while its tail is short and thin. The asp moves in long, slow, wavelike motions. Its body forms large S-shaped loops as it seems to flow along the ground.

A TIMID VIPER

The asp is a shy creature and will not attack people unless it is disturbed. But if someone steps on it by accident, it will defend itself, and it can be dangerous. The asp has two hollow fangs which it uses to inject poison, or venom, into its victims. If a person is bitten by an asp, he or she should be treated by a doctor as soon as possible.

Most snakes eat birds, lizards, and small rodents. When an asp attacks an animal, it first bites it with its fangs to poison it, then waits for its prey to die. It can swallow its victims whole because its jaws open very wide and its stomach expands to make room for the meal.

The danger that the asp poses to people is relatively minor. For instance, in

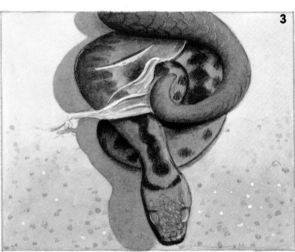

The asp is ovoviviparous: the eggs (1) hatch inside the mother (2) before the young asps are born (3).

France, four people died in five years (from 1979-1983) from asp bites. During that same time, ninety-six French people died from wasp, hornet, or bee stings. Because people are generally afraid of snakes, they often try to kill them. So many asps have been killed in France that there are now laws to protect them in that country.

MYTHS AND REALITY

Of all the animals on earth, snakes have the worst reputation. When they are mentioned, people usually react with fear or disgust.

Throughout history, the subject of snakes has given rise to myths and superstitions. For instance, it is said that the asp can hypnotize birds with its stare. This is not true. It does seem as if snakes stare for long periods of time but that is because they do not blink. Their eyes are covered with clear scales. They have no eyelids.

Sometimes we say that people who lie and say cruel things about others speak with a "viper's tongue." But that is quite unfair, since the viper's tongue does no harm. Snakes do not bite with their tongues, but with their fangs. The snake's tongue is, instead, the center for its sense of smell.

It is also said that the asp climbs trees, that it stands up on its tail, that it whistles when it is angry. And it is not uncommon to hear country folk in Europe say that the asps come out at night

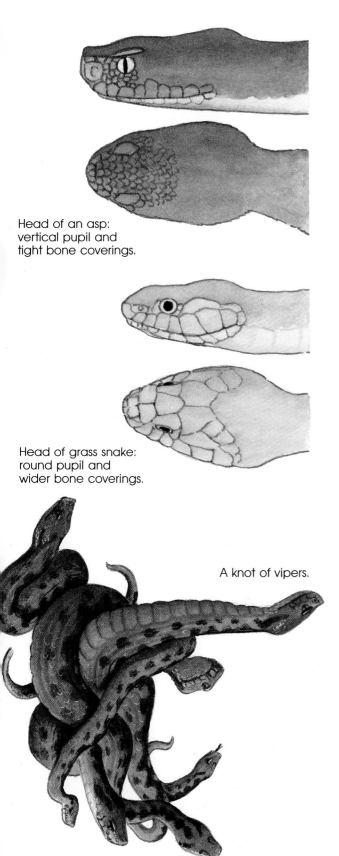

Head of an asp:
vertical pupil and
tight bone coverings.

Head of grass snake:
round pupil and
wider bone coverings.

A knot of vipers.

and milk the cows. But none of these sayings are true. They are only myths and superstitions.

Perhaps the most frightening myth about asps is the one that says an asp can catch a person who is running at top speed. In reality, the asp can crawl only in a horizontal position, and its greatest speed is about five miles an hour.

VIPER KNOTS

During cold weather asps sleep, or hibernate. They do so underground, beneath stones, or in hollow tree trunks. Often many asps will hibernate together in what are called "nests of vipers."

During the first sunny weeks of April, all the asps within a certain radius (of maybe 500 or 600 feet) begin to move at once. They seem to be following some mysterious signal, but actually they are responding to the scent which the other asps are sending out. Sometimes hundreds of asps can be seen moving together toward the same place. Their goal may be a pile of stones, a railroad embankment, a very sunny field. When the asps have gathered together, they begin to intertwine their bodies with one another. With several of their long bodies joined together, they look like large knots. In fact, they are called "viper knots." The knots keep changing in size and form as different snakes come together and move apart. This is the asps' mating ceremony.

THE EUROPEAN ROE DEER

ELEGANT AND SPIRITED

The roe deer is the smallest member of the deer family living in Europe. It is known for its graceful and nimble movements. It prefers living in woods that have thickets and many young saplings.

Deer have long, thin legs and can run very fast. The roe deer can run more than 48 miles an hour and leap as far as six feet. This elegant-looking animal has a long, thin neck, a narrow head, big eyes and large, horn-shaped ears.

The color of the roe deer changes with the seasons. It is brown-red in summer, brown-gray in winter. This change in coloring helps it to blend in with the background color of the changing seasons.

The roe deer's tail is very short, unlike that of the white-tailed deer, a deer commonly found in North America. The white-tailed deer has a tail about a foot long; the roe deer's is hardly recognizable as a tail at all. Beneath it there is a white spot which is especially visible in winter.

The female roe deer usually gives birth to two spotted fawns. She chooses a place hidden away from other deer. After they are born, the fawns remain in the hiding place for several weeks before they are able to follow their mother about in the forest.

It is not easy to spot a fawn in the woods because its color blends in so well with the background. But if you should happen to find one, be sure not to disturb it. Its mother is nearby and watching.

The roe deer can leap several yards at a time.

Most male deer are called bucks, but the male roe deer is called a brocket. It is easy to tell the male from the female because the male has antlers on its head, and the female does not. Each year, the antlers are shed. They grow back, stronger and more beautiful, the next year. When the new antlers are growing out, they are covered with a very thin skin, called velvet. Later, when the antlers are full grown, the deer will rub them against trees to scrape off the velvet.

The brocket uses its antlers to dig deep, vertical cuts in the trunks of trees. In this way it marks its territory. It also uses its antlers to fight with other males over mates.

IF YOU SEE A DEER

Often deer run away when they sense danger. Because they are so quick, they are able to escape from enemies in this way. But sometimes a deer will stand perfectly still and wait until the danger has passed. If you surprise a deer in the woods, it may stay very still, watching you. Or it may go bounding off noisily through the underbrush.

THE DEER'S TERRITORY

Deer don't have permanent homes, but they do have a selected territory in which they roam. This is where they find food, look for mates, and feel relatively safe from enemies. Deer eat twigs, leaves, tree buds, grass, moss, and sometimes grain from farmers' fields. In forests, trees and grasses provide plenty of food for deer. Bushes and shrubs make good hiding places from enemies and are safe places to give birth.

1) A brocket " in velvet."
2) The antler of the roe deer grows 5 to 7 inches in length.
3) Hoofprints of a roe deer.
4) A tree against which a roe deer has rubbed its antlers.

Although deer have large eyes, they rely mostly on their sense of smell and hearing to detect signs of danger. They usually face into the wind when they are eating or resting. In that way, if an enemy comes near, they will be able to see it or smell it. So if you should come upon a deer in the woods, be very quiet. Remember to stay downwind from it so it will not detect your presence. Then watch it closely.

SIGNS OF DEER

The best times to look for deer are in the early mornings or evenings. They are creatures of habit and often follow the same paths and eat in the same foraging areas. If you're looking for signs of deer, look for well-worn paths in the woods, trees where bark has been rubbed away, hoofprints, or piles of droppings along a path.

THE FOREST NUTHATCH

A CLIMBING ACROBAT

The nuthatch is a tree climber and usually lives in the forest. It can also be seen in town parks, often even in wooded gardens. It builds its nest in holes in trees and old stumps.

The nuthatch is about the size of a sparrow. It has a stocky body and a short tail. When the nuthatch is at rest, its head forms a straight line with its back, giving it a unique silhouette.

The nuthatch in the picture is one commonly found in Europe. It has a blue-gray back and a yellow-orange breast. The best-known kind, or species, of nuthatch in North America is the white-breasted nuthatch. It has a dark gray back. The upper parts of its head and neck are black, and, as its name suggests, its breast is white.

The nuthatch is one of the few birds that is able to climb down a tree head-first. Its very strong legs and powerful claws enable it to perform such acrobatic feats. It does not need to use its tail for help in keeping its balance.

A SEDENTARY BIRD

Some birds migrate, or travel south to spend the winter in warmer climates, but the nuthatch does not. It lives all year round in the same area if it can find enough food. In winter, when food is scarce, the nuthatch may leave its preferred home in the woods and move to nearby orchards and people's yards in search of food.

As early as March a pair of nuthatches begins to look for a nest — an old, abandoned woodpecker's nest, a hole in a stone wall, or perhaps a birdhouse.

As soon as the female nuthatch is through laying her eggs, she sits on them to keep them warm. The male brings food to her. During this time, the birds do not sing.

WHO IS KNOCKING ON THE TREE?

On an April morning, the forest echoes with a continuous sound: "toc-toc-toc." It comes from a nearby tree. One would expect to see a large bird there because the sound is so sharp and powerful. But it is the nuthatch which is making the noise as it uses its beak to try to get worms out of the tree bark.

The nuthatch feeds on insects, hazelnuts, beechnuts, or grain. It gets its name from the way it cracks open nuts. It wedges them in the cracks of tree bark and then uses its beak to shell them by striking them open (hatching).

The nuthatch cracks open a lot more nuts than it can eat and leaves the leftovers on many different tree trunks in its territory. Perhaps it will find them again during the winter. Without seeming to tire, the nuthatch spends its day flying from tree to tree, searching through its different "pantries" for food.

In winter, the nuthatch often visits bird feeders, looking for suet, sunflower seeds, and nuts. It knows how to fight for a place among the pushy titmice.

First the nuthatch wedges a nut between the cracks in tree bark. Then it cracks open the nut with its strong beak and eats it.

A mixture of seeds and suet attracts nuthatches and titmice.

AN ARTIFICIAL NEST

The nuthatch is a hole-nester. It sometimes makes its nest in birdhouses hung from trees. The birdhouse must be hung at least nine feet above the ground. It should be tied securely in place with strong rope. It must hang high off the ground to be out of reach of animals, especially cats.

If the opening is too wide, the nuthatch will plaster mud around it to make it narrower.

COMPETING FOR A NEST

The author of this book watched as a pair of nuthatches tried to take over the nest of some black woodpeckers. The woodpeckers were about the size of small crows. With their beaks, the woodpeckers pecked away at the tree, widening the hole little by little. Then they would leave for a while to look for food.

While they were gone, the nuthatches would plaster mud at the opening of the nest, which was too large for them. When the woodpeckers returned, they would chase the nuthatches away. Then the woodpeckers would begin to peck away at the hardened mud. When they departed again, the nuthatches would return and continue their work.

After the black woodpeckers had destroyed the nuthatches' mud entranceway three times, the nuthatches finally decided to abandon that nest site.

Although it usually lives in forests, the nuthatch may become a familiar sight in people's backyards. It will eat from bird feeders and may nest in birdhouses.

ANTS

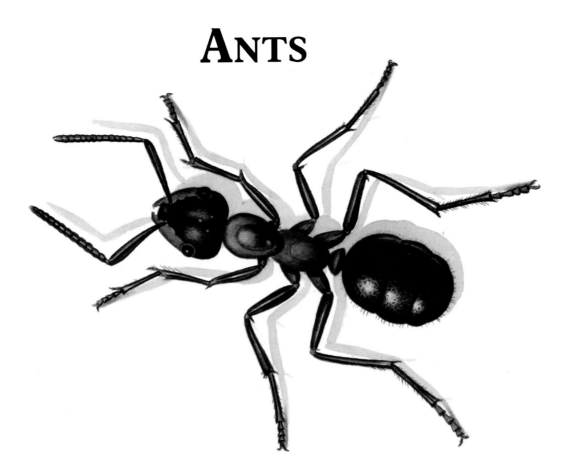

AN ORGANIZED SOCIETY

Ants are social insects. That means they live together in groups and depend on one another to survive. Groups of ants are often called colonies.

Many kinds, or species, of ants make their nests underground. These nests are made up of many tunnels and rooms. The rooms are used for storing food, caring for the eggs and young (or larvae), and for gathering together and resting. There is even a special room for the queen ant. Some ants, such as those shown here, pile soil, twigs and pine needles over their underground nests. This type of nest is called an anthill.

Other ants do not build much of a nest at all. Instead, they will nest beneath a pile of dead wood, in a mound of grass-covered soil, or even in hollowed trees or house beams.

Life in the ant colony is very organized. In most colonies, there are three types of ants: workers, males and queens. Each type, or class, has certain duties. Most ants in a colony are worker ants. The worker ants care for the queen, build and defend the nest, care for the young, and gather food. Male ants do no work in the colony. They live only a short time, and their only job is to mate with the queen. Then there are the queen ants, which are usually larger than the others. The colony may have one or several queens. The life-long job of the queen ant is to lay eggs.

AN ARTIFICIAL ANTHILL

Scientists or other observers sometimes build glass cages like the one pictured here to study ants. These glass cages are called artificial anthills. With an artificial anthill, the observer can learn about life in an underground nest. Projects like this need a lot of care. Ants are very small. They can escape through the smallest crack or opening.

To build an artificial anthill, you must first find a real one. When you do, take soil from several of the nest's different levels. Use a shovel or trowel. Make sure there are ants in the soil. To start a colony, you will need worker ants, ant larvae, and at least one queen ant. It is also important that all of the ants come from the same ant colony. All ants from one colony have a special odor. So the ants "recognize" one another by the smell. They will also "recognize" any ant that is from a different colony. Ants from separate colonies may fight or even kill one another. In order to avoid this, do not mix the ants.

Put the ants, soil and some twigs in the new anthill. In a few days, the ants will begin their new nest. They will build the different levels and dig rooms for storing their food, for their larvae, and for their queen.

FOOD COLLECTORS

Ants find their own food in the wild. Finding food is the only job that some ants have.

An artificial anthill.

Collecting ants.

40

Male winged ant ready to mate.

Queen

Worker ant

The worker ants care for the eggs and larvae.

An artificial anthill can be any size. But it must have two separate rooms.

1) Air holes covered with very thin wire netting or screen.
2) Holes between the anthill and the food.
3) Watering place.
4) Holes to add food.

Add water to the soil in the nest.

When they find it, they rush back to the nest to tell the others. Ants "talk" by touching each other's feelers, or antennae. The antennae are jointed and bend easily in many directions. Ants use them for many things, including "talking". Soon all the ants know of the discovery. Many workers rush from the nest to find the food, guided by each other's scent. A great two-way line is formed between the nest and the food. The ants scurry back and forth along the trail, carrying pieces of food that are sometimes larger than they are.

Another favorite food of certain ant species is the sweet liquid known as honeydew. Honeydew comes from very small insects known as aphids. Aphids feed on certain types of plants, sucking the juices from them. Ants visit the plants where the aphids feed, looking for the honeydew. When the ants stroke the aphids on the back with their antennae, the aphids excrete the honeydew from their abdomens, or back part of their bodies. The ants are sometimes said to be "milking" the aphids.

In turn, the ants protect the aphids from their insect enemies such as ladybugs or lacewings. Some ant species actually keep the aphid eggs in their nests during the winter. When the eggs hatch in the spring, the ants will then take them from the nest back to their favorite plants. Through this helping relationship, the ants are sure to always have a supply of honeydew.

THE GREY CUCKOO

THE CUCKOO'S SONG

Cuckoo is the name of several related birds. The cuckoo family gets its name from the pleasing song of the European cuckoo. The grey cuckoo, pictured here, is a European cuckoo. In North America, there are two common types of cuckoo birds. They are the black-billed cuckoo and the yellow-billed cuckoo.

Cuckoos are shy birds and not often seen. They live in the woods, thickets and orchards. But it is always easy to tell when a cuckoo is near by its loud call. In early April, the cuckoo may be heard echoing through the forests. That is when the cuckoo comes to look for a mate. Except for this short mating season, the grey cuckoo likes to live alone.

The grey cuckoo is ash grey in color. Even its white breast is striped with grey. Sometimes it is mistaken for another bird, known as the sparrow-hawk. The two birds are similar in size and color. But the cuckoo bird has feet very different from those of most birds. Like its American cousins, the grey cuckoo has feet with two toes pointing forward and two toes pointing backward. This and its sweet song set the cuckoo bird apart from other birds.

Cuckoo birds feed on insects. Some types of hairy caterpillars are among its favorite foods. Many other birds will not eat the caterpillars that the cuckoo eats. They find its hair irritating. This does not bother the cuckoo. Still, because it is an insect-eater, the cuckoo must migrate to warmer places in the winter.

THE CLEVER CUCKOO

The grey cuckoo is called a parasite of other birds. That means that it depends on others to help it but gives nothing in return. The cuckoo is a parasite because it does not take care of its own young. Instead, it lays its eggs in other birds' nests and leaves them to be raised by the other bird.

When it is time to lay eggs, the female cuckoo searches for other nearby bird nests. She instinctively chooses the same species of bird each time. Usually it is the same kind of bird that raised her. The cuckoo then waits for her chance. The minute the other bird leaves her nest — even for a moment — in swoops the cuckoo. She only needs a few seconds to lay her egg. Then she is off to find another nest for another egg.

ALWAYS THE FIRST

The cuckoo bird has adapted to growing up in an "adoptive" nest. The cuckoo egg usually hatches sooner than the eggs of its host. Sometimes it does hatch at the same time as the rest. In either case, the cuckoo bird survives. Instinctively, the young cuckoo will throw the other eggs or the fledglings born before it over the nest edge. Often the cuckoo does this immediately after it is born. Strangely, the parent birds are not upset by this. They feed and raise the cuckoo as their own.

In some weeks, the cuckoo will grow ten times bigger than its adoptive parents. By then it is very hard work to

The female cuckoo lays its egg . . .

. . . and abandons it.

The young cuckoo throws the other eggs from the nest.

keep up with the young cuckoo's appetite. They are kept busy all day long.

In no time, the cuckoo outgrows the nest, too. It breaks under the weight, dumping the cuckoo. On the ground or in the branches, the cuckoo continues to call for food for awhile. Eventually, it will leave its "parents" and begin its life alone as a cuckoo.

Cuckoo birds go to much trouble to have other birds raise their young. They are not always successful. Some of the other birds reject the cuckoo eggs. The black-headed hedge sparrow throws the cuckoo eggs out of its nest. The willow warbler just abandons the nest. Perhaps only one egg out of fifteen or twenty laid by the female cuckoo will reach adulthood.

A WORD WITH MANY MEANINGS

The cuckoo bird has always fascinated people. Its song and its beauty have inspired both legends and traditions. Certainly many people are familiar with the cuckoo clock and its sad, two-note song. And according to one legend, "Whoever has a small amount of money when the cuckoo first sings will be rich for all the year."

The cuckoo has also influenced our language. According to the dictionary, "cuckoo" means: a fowl whose feathers look like the cuckoo's, the wild French daffodil, a wooden cuckoo clock, an old car, a locomotive for moving railroad cars, a plane in military slang, a fool, etc. Can you think of others?

"Whoever has a small amount of money when the cuckoo first sings, will be rich for all the year."

FACTS AT A GLANCE

Scientific classification is a method of identifying and organizing all living things. Using this method, scientists place plants and animals in groups according to similar characteristics. Characteristics are traits or qualities that make one organism different from another.

There are seven major breakdowns, or groups, to this method of classification. They include: kingdom, phylum, class, order, family, genus, and species. The kingdom is the largest group. It contains the most kinds of animals or plants. For example, all animals belong to the animal kingdom, Animalia. The species is the smallest of the groupings. Members of a species are alike in many ways. They are also different from all other living things in one or more ways.

THE MARTEN

Phylum:	**Chordata** (vertebrates)
Class:	**Mammalia** (mammals)
Order:	**Carnivora** (flesh-eating)
Size:	27 to 28 inches long
Reproduction:	One or two litters of 3 to 6 per year
Habitat:	Mountains and forests of Europe, Asia, and North America
Diet:	Rodents (especially squirrels), birds, insects, berries

THE BOAR

Phylum:	**Chordata** (vertebrates)
Class:	**Mammalia** (mammals)
Order:	**Artiodactyla** (even-toed, hoofed animals)
Size:	31 inches high at shoulders, 59 inches long
Reproduction:	2 to 12 striped young per year
Habitat:	Forests, swamps and rocky areas, etc. Found in Asia, North Africa and throughout Europe, except for Scandinavia.
Diet:	Rodents, reptiles, bulbs, leaves, fruit, snails

THE HAWK

Phylum:	**Chordata** (vertebrates)
Class:	**Aves** (birds)
Order:	**Falconiformes** (daytime birds of prey)
Size:	19 to 23 inches long; wingspan of 3½ to 4 feet
Reproduction:	2 to 6 eggs per year
Habitat:	Woods, cultivated areas, and plains of most continents
Diet:	Rodents, snakes, lizards, frogs, insects, fish.

BARK BEETLES

Phylum:	**Arthropoda** (joint-footed animal)
Class:	**Insecta** (insects)
Order:	**Coleoptera** (sheath-winged)
Size:	Less than ¼ of an inch long
Reproduction:	Four-stage development metamorphosis (egg, larva, pupa, adult)
Habitat:	Tunnels in living or dead wood
Diet:	Feeds on or in wood